MW01536774

Original title:
Garden of Light

Author: Sebastian Sarapuu
ISBN HARDBACK: 978-9908-1-2257-1
ISBN PAPERBACK: 978-9908-1-2258-8
ISBN EBOOK: 978-9908-1-2259-5

Soft Hues of Dawn

The sun peeks over hills so high,
Painting skies in a gentle sigh.
Warmth drapes softly on waking trees,
Whispers of joy carried by the breeze.

Birds burst forth in sweet delight,
Their songs weaving into morning light.
Colors blend in a festive array,
Dancing bright, heralding the day.

Prismatic Blooms

Petals unfurl in vibrant cheer,
Nature's palette, vivid and clear.
Butterflies flutter, a playful sight,
Amidst the blooms, pure delight.

Laughter echoes in sunny realms,
Children play, each joy overwhelms.
Colors collide in joyful display,
A festive scene in bright bouquet.

Flourish of Glow

Lanterns flicker, casting gold,
Embers dance, stories unfold.
Families gather, sharing their tales,
Life's tapestry, woven in trails.

Under twinkling stars, spirits rise,
Laughter sparkles in joyous skies.
A chorus of hearts, so light and free,
In this flourish, together we be.

The Glinting Sanctuary

A haven where joy knows no end,
Friendship blooms, hearts to mend.
Laughter fills every vibrant space,
The world transformed into a warm embrace.

Twinkling lights adorn each wall,
Echoes of happiness, a captivating call.
In this glinting sanctuary, we unite,
Celebrating life, our spirits ignite.

Illuminated Blossoms

In gardens bright, where colors play,
The flowers dance in bright array.
With laughter sweet, the breezes sway,
A symphony of light's bouquet.

Each petal shines in golden rays,
As joy and cheer weave through the days.
Together, hearts in blissful praise,
We celebrate this vibrant phase.

Radiance in Bloom

The sunlit skies, all warm and clear,
Bring forth the blooms we hold so dear.
With every hue, our hearts draw near,
United in this time of cheer.

A fragrant breeze, a joyous sound,
In every corner, life is found.
With laughter shared, the world surrounds,
In vibrant shades, our love is crowned.

Celestial Petals

Through starlit nights and moonlit gleams,
The flowers bloom like sweet dreams.
With every whisper, magic seems,
To weave enchantment in our themes.

The twinkle lights in soft embrace,
As petals blush, our cares erase.
In festive joy, we find our place,
Together dancing, oh, what grace!

Luminous Visions

With fireworks bright in the evening sky,
We gather close, our spirits fly.
Each sparkle shines, a twinkling sigh,
In festive glow, we dream and try.

As colors merge, our hopes ignite,
In joyful hearts, we find the light.
With every beat, our souls take flight,
Embracing love, all through the night.

A Symphony of Color

In the air, a melody bright,
Every hue dances with delight,
Children laugh, their joy takes flight,
Painting the world in sheer sunlight.

Flags wave high, a joyful parade,
With each step, fresh memories made,
Colors blend in a grand cascade,
Life's canvas by laughter displayed.

Echoes of Pure Light

A lantern's glow in the night sky,
Whispers of hope as breezes sigh,
Stars awaken, twinkling high,
Under a tapestry, dreams can fly.

Voices unite in harmony sweet,
With each beat, rich joy replete,
Dancing shadows to a festive beat,
In this moment, our hearts meet.

The Spectral Grove

Among the trees, an echo rings,
Nature dons its festive strings,
Leaves shimmer like gold and wings,
As laughter in the breeze softly clings.

Beneath the boughs, we weave our dreams,
Bright colors blend in joyful schemes,
Magic lingers in light's beams,
In the grove, nothing's as it seems.

Dazzling Petal Dance

Petals swirl in an eager breeze,
Painting the ground with vibrant ease,
Nature's rhythm brings hearts to tease,
As blooms sway in the dance of trees.

Each flower nods, a gentle sway,
In this garden where spirits play,
Colors burst, come what may,
In a festive dance, we lose the gray.

Lumen Blossoms

In gardens bright with colors bold,
The laughter dances, stories told.
Petals twirl in the cheerful breeze,
A celebration among the trees.

Candles flicker, shadows play,
Hearts filled with joy, come what may.
Voices soar like birds in flight,
Together we bask in the warm daylight.

The Dazzling Foliage

Leaves aglow in golden light,
Whispers of fall, a splendid sight.
Beneath the boughs, the children gleam,
In nature's arms, they'll dance and dream.

Glimmers shimmer like stars at night,
Bubbles rise with pure delight.
Every step, a joyful sound,
In this festooned world we've found.

Ethereal Lightfall

As twilight falls, a canvas bright,
Colors swirl in an endless flight.
Fireflies twinkle, a soft serenade,
In the night's embrace, dreams are made.

Laughter echoes through the trees,
Spirits lifted on a gentle breeze.
Moments weave into a festive glow,
In this magic, we all ebb and flow.

Harmonies of the Day

Morning breaks with lively cheer,
Voices blend, the world draws near.
Banners wave in the sunlit air,
An anthem of joy, beyond compare.

Together we dance in vibrant throngs,
Each heartbeat sings in merry songs.
Life unfolds in splendid array,
In the harmonies of the day.

Whispers of Radiance

In the garden, laughter flows,
Colors dance where soft wind blows.
Radiant blooms in shades so bright,
Celebrations spark the night.

Banners flutter, voices soar,
Joyful hearts find room for more.
Twinkling lights above they rise,
Illuminating smiling eyes.

Together we embrace the cheer,
As festive songs draw loved ones near.
In each moment, love ignites,
Whispers of radiant delights.

Blossoms Beneath the Sun

Beneath the sun, the petals sway,
Nature's charm leads hearts to play.
Golden rays in blue skies shine,
Festive spirits intertwine.

Children laugh and run about,
Filling every heart with doubt.
For in this joy, they find their place,
A world adorned in sweet embrace.

The scent of blooms fills the air,
Gathered friends, a bond so rare.
Every moment, tendrils twine,
Blossoms beneath the sun align.

Luminescent Serenity

Moonlit nights bring gentle peace,
Where laughter and joy never cease.
Glowing hearts with warmth align,
In this quiet, stars brightly shine.

Candles flicker, shadows dance,
Creating echoes of romance.
Each voice a note in harmony,
Luminescent soul's decree.

Beneath starry skies, we share,
Moments cherished, light as air.
In serenity, we find the way,
A festive tune where dreams still play.

Petals in the Dawn

As dawn breaks with golden hue,
Petals awaken, kissed by dew.
Hope unfurls in blossomed grace,
Delight found in nature's face.

With every ray, a new day calls,
Joyfulness in laughter sprawls.
Families gather, hugs so tight,
Hearts aglow with purest light.

Beneath the sky, together we'll roam,
Each step a whisper of home.
In the promise of the morn,
Petals in the dawn reborn.

The Radiant Canopy

Under a sky of vibrant hue,
Laughter dances, spirits anew.
Balloons afloat in sunlit beams,
Joy unfurls in colorful dreams.

Families gather, stories unfold,
With every hug, warm hands to hold.
Festive tables laden with cheer,
Delights and feasts, we hold dear.

Twinkling lights, they wink and gleam,
In this moment, we're part of a dream.
Music swells, voices harmonize,
As love binds us beneath the skies.

Together we weave a tapestry bright,
Celebrating moments that feel just right.
The radiant canopy envelops all,
In this joyful embrace, we stand tall.

Harmony in the Light

Candles twinkle, casting soft glow,
Melodies linger, setting the flow.
Each note a whisper, pure and sweet,
Footsteps move to the rhythmic beat.

In harmony, we share this night,
Friends and kin, hearts shining bright.
Together we'll dance, we'll sing,
In the warmth of love that we bring.

Laughter entwined with the stars so high,
As wishes take wing and gently fly.
Under the moon's gentle embrace,
We find joy in this sacred space.

Here, hope blooms like flowers in spring,
In this dance of life, our voices ring.
Harmony in the light, takes flight,
As we bask in the glow of the night.

Candlelight of the Wild

Beneath the canopy of trees so grand,
A flickering flame, a wish in hand.
Whispers of nature echo the call,
In the candlelight, we cherish it all.

Stars above, like diamonds bright,
Cast a magic upon the night.
Gathered round with stories to share,
Bonded in laughter, hearts laid bare.

Fireflies dance in a playful flight,
Guiding our spirits in sheer delight.
With every spark, we find our way,
In this wild embrace, we choose to stay.

The night is ours, in warmth we bask,
Trust in this moment, it's all we ask.
Candlelight flickers, softly shines,
In nature's embrace, love aligns.

Enchanted by Daybreak

Morning unfolds with a golden hue,
The world awakens, refreshed and new.
Birds serenade with songs of cheer,
In the soft light, joy draws near.

Fields shimmer with dew's gentle kiss,
Each moment whispers of simple bliss.
Children's laughter, a sweet refrain,
In this magic, there's nothing to gain.

Colors burst as the sun climbs high,
Painting the sky, oh how we sigh!
Together we bask in nature's grace,
Chasing the shadows, we find our place.

In unity, we rise and play,
Enchanted by the promise of day.
With hearts aligned, we embrace the sun,
Together in joy, forever begun.

Twilight's Luminous Call

In the evening glow, we gather near,
Laughter dances, filling the air.
Stars awaken, their sparkles bright,
Celebrate the magic of the night.

Candles flicker, their light divine,
Hearts pulse with joy, like sweet red wine.
Whispers of dreams, in laughter we share,
Together we weave this festive affair.

The moonrise brings a gentle cheer,
As melodies float, all worries disappear.
In this twilight, our spirits soar,
Gathered in love, forevermore.

Midnight approaches, the dance unfolds,
Wrapped in warmth, as the night beholds.
With every twirl, we chase the stars,
In twilight's glow, we heal our scars.

Shades of Dawn

Morning breaks with a joyful hue,
Soft whispers greet the world anew.
Colors blooming, warm and bright,
Fragrant flowers dance in light.

Birds chirp sweetly, a vibrant song,
Nature's chorus, where we belong.
Sunrise kisses the dew-kissed grass,
In this moment, all sorrows pass.

Families gather, laughter cascades,
Love is the thread that never fades.
With every hug, our spirits rise,
In shades of dawn, our hearts unite.

Celebrations greet the breaking day,
Joyful smiles chase the night away.
In the warmth of this golden glow,
Together we share the love we sow.

Celestial Canopy

Beneath the stars, the laughter rings,
Colors dance, as joy takes wing.
A tapestry of dreams unfolds,
In the night, tales of old.

Flickering lights in harmony play,
Whispers of magic on this bright day.
With hearts aglow, we share this night,
Bound together in sheer delight.

Softly Swaying Glimmers

Twinkling lights in the silent air,
Glistening smiles through shimmering hair.
Embraced by warmth, the world ignites,
Joy dances freely, the spirit excites.

Children laugh as they run around,
In every corner, enchantment's found.
With each step, the music flows,
In this haven, our spirits grow.

The Lightweaver's Nook

Here in the corner where dreams align,
Magic weaves with a thread divine.
Charming whispers in glowing tones,
Craft tales of wonder, as life condones.

The laughter echoes, a melody sweet,
Wrapped in joy, where friends all meet.
In every moment, the love shines bright,
In this nook, we embrace the night.

Radiant Echoes

Bright colors flare as voices clash,
In joyous chorus, the moments flash.
Radiant echoes of love resound,
In every heartbeat, together we're found.

With every cheer, our spirits soar,
In the warmth of laughter, we crave for more.
Hand in hand, we dance through the glow,
In the tapestry of life, we forever flow.

The Brilliant Tapestry

Colors bright in joyful dance,
Laughter spills, a playful chance,
Glimmers twinkle in the air,
Hearts unite, a moment rare.

Banners wave in warm embrace,
Folk gather in their lively space,
Music plays, the drums ignite,
Underneath the moon's soft light.

Gifts of joy, we share them wide,
Festive dreams, they swell our pride,
Stories shared from days of old,
In this tapestry of gold.

As the night begins to fade,
Memories in laughter laid,
Friends and family side by side,
In this warmth, we take our stride.

Fields of Resplendence

Fields alive with vibrant hues,
Dancing sunbeams, morning's muse,
Blossoms sway and freely bloom,
Nature's scent dispels the gloom.

Breezes carry joyful songs,
Where the heart of life belongs,
Colors splash in every view,
Waves of joy, sweet as the dew.

Gather 'round, the feast awaits,
Cherished moments, open gates,
Under skies, so brilliantly clear,
We embrace what we hold dear.

Laughter echoes, spirits high,
As the stars begin to fly,
Fields of dreams, our hearts expand,
In this resplendence, we stand.

Radiant Whispers

Whispers soft as twilight hum,
Echo in the hearts that come,
In the air, a spell is cast,
Moments cherished, friendships vast.

Candles twinkle, shadows play,
Illuminating our array,
Stories shared by fire's glow,
In this warmth, love starts to grow.

Sparkling eyes and laughter bright,
Every voice a pure delight,
In the circle, joy does swirl,
Radiant whispers, hopes unfurl.

As the night unfolds its dreams,
Together bask in silver beams,
Hand in hand, the world feels near,
In this magic, hearts adhere.

Nature's Illuminated Canvas

Nature paints with vivid brush,
In each color, hearts do hush,
Leaves a'glitter in the breeze,
Whispers carried through the trees.

Sunset hues of orange glint,
Sparkling gold, a joyous tint,
Every moment pure and bright,
Canvas rich in sheer delight.

Gathered here, the songs resound,
Harmony in love profound,
As the stars come out to play,
We celebrate this vibrant day.

With each brushstroke, life weaves tight,
Joy and laughter, sheer delight,
In this canvas, we find grace,
Nature's love, our warm embrace.

Glistening Tranquility

In the glow of twinkling lights,
Laughter dances in the air,
Joy unfolds in gentle sighs,
Whispers soft, a tender care.

Snowflakes fall like feathery dreams,
Blanketing the world in white,
Children's giggles blend with gleams,
As hearts are warmed by pure delight.

Candles flicker, casting spells,
Every corner filled with cheer,
Stories shared, each tale compels,
A festive spirit drawing near.

With each toast, we lift our glass,
To moments cherished, held so dear,
In this light, all worries pass,
Glistening tranquility is here.

Harvest of Dreams

Crisp leaves falling, gold and red,
Gathered round for warmth and feasts,
Stories shared and good hearts spread,
A season blessed, joy's not the least.

Pumpkins glowing on each step,
Candied treats in every hand,
While laughter weaves a vibrant web,
We celebrate this bountiful land.

The cornucopia's vibrant hues,
A tapestry of nature's grace,
Together, we shall all imbue,
A harvest dream time can't erase.

Let's raise our voices, sing and sway,
In gratitude, we find our theme,
For in this moment, we will play,
United in this harvest dream.

Flickers in the Canopy

Beneath the stars, a wondrous sight,
Fireflies dance, a fleeting glow,
As branches sway, the heart takes flight,
In nature's arms, time moves slow.

Each whisper of the evening breeze,
Carries laughter, soft and bright,
Like melodies among the trees,
We cherish every spark of light.

With blankets spread on grassy ground,
We share our stories and our dreams,
In this embrace of night profound,
Where flickers weave through starlit beams.

Together here, we find our peace,
Connected by the warmth we glean,
In gentle moments, joy won't cease,
Flickers in the canopy seen.

Solstice Reverie

As daylight wanes, we gather close,
A circle formed, hearts beating free,
With candles lit, we feel the prose,
Of solstice dreams in harmony.

The air is crisp, with laughter bright,
A chorus of our souls' embrace,
We share our wishes, hopes in sight,
In this warm glow, we find our place.

Each story told, a treasured thread,
Stitched in memories, rich and rare,
With joy and love, our spirits spread,
A festive note fills all the air.

Together now, we dance and sing,
In this reverie, we will thrive,
For in the heart, a promise rings,
Solstice magic keeps us alive.

Echoes of Silver Moonlight

Beneath the stars, the laughter swells,
Sound of joy, the night compels.
Silver beams on dancing trees,
A serenade within the breeze.

Glistening hopes all intertwine,
In the glow, we sip the wine.
Fires crackle, stories shared,
Memories blossom, hearts prepared.

Candles flicker, shadows play,
In this realm, we cast away.
Every whisper, every cheer,
Echoes sweet as we draw near.

With each note, the music sways,
Carried forth in festive ways.
As silver moonlight graces time,
We find our rhythm, pure and prime.

The Light's Tender Caress

Morning breaks, the sun ascends,
Color blooms, the day transcends.
Golden rays through branches stream,
Warmth that fills the heart with dream.

Breezes dance through fields of green,
Nature sings, a vibrant scene.
Voices rise, in harmonies,
Joyful hearts like whispered bees.

Every smile, a ray of gold,
Hearts unite, both young and old.
In this moment, we embrace,
Life's sweet gift, the light's grace.

Cakes and laughter fill the air,
With each bite, we savor care.
For in this glow, we find our way,
Together, in this festive play.

Whispers of the Dawn

As the night begins to fade,
Color softens, dreams cascade.
Awake with joy, the world ignites,
A canvas blooms in morning lights.

Birds will sing, their melodies,
Like gentle thoughts upon the breeze.
With every chirp, the heart will soar,
A symphony of glee once more.

Sunrise paints the sky in hues,
Each heartbeat shares the vibrant news.
Gather friends, this day is ours,
In the splendor of the stars.

Together we weave the threads of grace,
In laughter's warmth, find our place.
For in these whispers, soft yet strong,
We celebrate, where we belong.

Aurora's Embrace

In twilight meld where colors blend,
A spectacle that knows no end.
The aurora dances, vivid and bright,
Welcoming all with pure delight.

Each hue a joy, a vibrant thread,
Painting skies overhead.
Under this canopy, we gather tight,
Kaleidoscopes of dreams take flight.

In laughter's echo, stars ignite,
Wishes form in the starry night.
Joyful hearts, a shared embrace,
Together we find a sacred space.

Moments woven with threads of cheer,
As the night draws near, we persevere.
In the glow of aurora's art,
We feel the magic in every heart.

A Symphony of Sunbeams

Dancing rays in morning light,
Whispers of joy take flight.
Children laugh, hearts align,
Nature sings, pure and divine.

Colorful blooms in every glance,
In the breeze, we sway and dance.
Joyful echoes fill the air,
Together we shed every care.

From rooftops high to meadows low,
Sun-kissed memories start to flow.
With every smile, the world ignites,
In the warmth of endless nights.

A festive spirit, bright and free,
United in sweet harmony.
As sunbeams weave their playful art,
A symphony that fills the heart.

Shimmering Vistas

Golden fields stretch far and wide,
Where laughter and love collide.
Balloons soar in azure skies,
With every wave, our spirits rise.

Chasing moments, we embrace,
In every smile, a warm trace.
Picnics spread on grassy beds,
Where joyful stories weave life's threads.

Fireflies twinkle, a magical sight,
As friends gather under the light.
With shimmering vistas all around,
Every heartbeat sings profound.

Festive laughter fills the night,
As stars emerge in brilliant white.
Together we hold the memories dear,
In this wonder, we have no fear.

Embrace of the Luminous

Glistening lights upon the trees,
An evening painted with gentle ease.
Families gather, stories unfold,
In the warmth, we find our gold.

Candles flicker, hearts align,
Under the stars, our souls entwine.
Songs of joy echo through the air,
In the embrace of love, we share.

Festive dreams weave through the night,
As laughter dances in soft light.
Hand in hand, we spin and twirl,
Creating magic in every swirl.

A tapestry of joy we weave,
A luminous bond we believe.
In the embrace of all things bright,
We shine together, pure delight.

Sunlit Reverie

The dawn awakens with a glow,
A gentle breeze begins to flow.
Children play in fields of green,
Sunlit dreams, a joyful scene.

Petals dance with laughter's cheer,
In every moment, we find dear.
With every ray, our hearts ignite,
In the warmth of golden light.

The world feels fairytale-like today,
As we chase our cares away.
Sunlit reverie fills the air,
In every hug, a love laid bare.

With friends and laughter all around,
In blissful joy, we are found.
In the heart of this radiant spree,
We celebrate, forever free.

Sunlit Reverie

In the glow of bright sunshine,
Laughter dances through the air,
Children play on the green grass,
Joy reflected everywhere.

Balloons float in the soft breeze,
Colors splashed against the blue,
Smiles shine like the golden rays,
Hearts are light, and spirits too.

Sweet treats line the wooden tables,
Cakes and pies for all to share,
Songs of joy fill every corner,
Love and laughter everywhere.

As the day turns into evening,
Fireflies twinkle like the stars,
We gather close and tell our stories,
Creating magic, near and far.

Glistening Horizons

Golden rays touch the horizon,
As daylight begins to fade,
A festive glow lights the pathways,
For a night of joy we've made.

Lanterns hang in happy clusters,
Casting warmth on smiling faces,
Friends and family come together,
Celebrating in warm embraces.

Laughter rings like sweet music,
Every heartbeat filled with cheer,
Stories shared around the fire,
Making memories held dear.

Dancing shadows greet the twilight,
As the stars begin to gleam,
With dreams woven in the night sky,
We drift softly into a dream.

Nature's Glowing Canvas

Fields adorned in vibrant colors,
Petals whispering to the breeze,
Sunsets paint the world in splendor,
A canvas bright, designed with ease.

Butterflies flit from bloom to bloom,
The air is sweet with nature's brew,
Each moment glows with pure delight,
In this paradise, all feels new.

Gathered 'neath the leafy branches,
Families share in simple joys,
Picnics spread upon the soft grass,
Filled with laughter, girls and boys.

As stars emerge in velvet skies,
We toast to dreams, both bold and true,
Nature's glow wraps 'round our hearts,
In this festive, magic view.

The Solstice Meadow

The solstice sun brings golden light,
To the meadow, lush and wide,
Families gather, spirits bright,
With joy and laughter as our guide.

Children chase the dancing shadows,
As flowers bloom like hearts anew,
The air is filled with song and laughter,
In a world where dreams come true.

Picnic baskets overflowing,
With every taste, a precious bite,
Under skies of azure blue,
We cherish this warm, festive night.

As fireflies flicker in the dusk,
We write our hopes upon the breeze,
This meadow filled with love and light,
Forever holding our memories.

Daybreak Tapestry

Colors blend in morning light,
A canvas spread, so warm and bright.
Laughter dances on the breeze,
Nature wakes with joyous ease.

Banners wave in golden sun,
Festive hearts, the day begun.
Joyful songs fill every space,
Smiles reflect on every face.

Children play with carefree glee,
Chasing dreams, feeling so free.
The world adorned in radiant hues,
A day to cherish, laugh, and muse.

As sunlight spills on dew-kissed ground,
In this daybreak, joy is found.
A tapestry of life unfolds,
In colors bright, our stories told.

Shining Meadows

Across the fields, the flowers sway,
In shimmering blooms, we greet the day.
Sunrise whispers, soft and clear,
A call to gather, far and near.

Picnic blankets on the grass,
As laughter echoes, moments pass.
Baskets filled with sweet delight,
We share our joys, from morn 'til night.

Kites are flying, spirits soar,
In this meadow, we explore.
With every step, we feel the beat,
As hearts entwine, we're feeling sweet.

As twilight paints the sky with gold,
Together we weave memories bold.
A fest of life, in every glance,
In shining meadows, we find romance.

Veils of Illumination

Stars emerge as dusk draws near,
Twinkling lights that bring us cheer.
Lanterns glow with warmth and grace,
In the night, we find our place.

The air is filled with sweet delight,
As shadows dance in soft moonlight.
Veils of joy, fluttering free,
In this moment, just you and me.

Spirits high, as stories share,
With laughter ringing in the air.
The world aglow with hope and dreams,
Tonight is magical, or so it seems.

United hearts, we raise a toast,
To the moments we cherish most.
Veils of illumination shine,
In this festive night, you are mine.

Illuminated Whispers

In secret corners, whispers bloom,
With tales that spark the night's perfume.
Candles flicker with soft delight,
Illuminated by joy tonight.

The table set with treasures bright,
A banquet shared in soft twilight.
Lively voices merge as one,
Celebrating all that we've begun.

Every glance holds magic's trace,
In this gathering, love's embrace.
With each moment, memories grow,
As radiant laughter starts to flow.

The night unfolds, a canvas wide,
In illuminated whispers, we confide.
Under stars, our dreams ignite,
A festive dance beneath the night.

Enchanted Sunbeams

Bright rays dance upon the ground,
Joyful laughter all around.
Children play with hearts so free,
Love and light, their jubilee.

Golden glimmers fill the air,
Nature's bounty, lovely rare.
Every smile sparks a cheer,
Whispers of the sun draw near.

Flowers bloom in vibrant hue,
Every petal kissed by dew.
Music plays from far and wide,
Enchanted moments coincide.

As day fades and stars appear,
Magic lingers, drawing near.
Festive hearts, together spun,
In the glow of setting sun.

The Verdant Awakening

In the meadow, colors bright,
Nature wakes with pure delight.
Dewy petals stretch and yawn,
A symphony of joyous dawn.

Buzzing bees, they flit and fly,
Painted butterflies drift by.
Every leaf a story tells,
In the air, enchantment dwells.

Laughter rings like silver bells,
Echoes of the tales it tells.
Children run through fields of green,
In this moment, pure and keen.

Underneath the vast blue sky,
Hearts unite as dreams soar high.
Together in this vivid scene,
A world awash in vibrant sheen.

Twilight's Caress

As the sun dips in the west,
Twilight whispers, soft and best.
Colors blend in warm embrace,
A tranquil smile lights the space.

Stars awaken, twinkling bright,
Crickets serenade the night.
Laughter dances in the breeze,
Joyful echoes through the trees.

Candles flicker, shadows sway,
Gathered friends in sweet array.
Every heart sings a new song,
In this moment, we belong.

Moonlight paints the world in dreams,
Golden glow in silvery streams.
Twilight's magic, gentle, fair,
Wraps us softly, everywhere.

Blooming Brilliance

Petals burst in colors bold,
Stories of the spring unfold.
Fragrant breezes floating by,
Nature's canvas in the sky.

Each blossom beams, a radiant light,
Filling hearts with pure delight.
Dancers sway, the garden's glee,
As the world calls joyfully.

Rainbows arch through skies so clear,
Every moment, magic near.
Underneath the sun's embrace,
Friendship flourishes in this place.

Together, let our spirits soar,
Celebration forevermore.
In blooming brilliance, we unite,
In love's warm and endless light.

Oasis of Radiance

In the midst of laughter bright,
Colors twirl in joyful flight.
Glowing hearts dance and sway,
Celebrating this grand day.

Bubbles rise like stars in night,
Joyful cheers take rapid flight.
Underneath the moon's embrace,
Smiles shine on every face.

Candles flicker with delight,
Sparks of hope take gentle flight.
Together we share this bliss,
In this moment, pure happiness.

With each toast and every cheer,
Friendships blossom, drawing near.
In this oasis, hearts expand,
Together we will always stand.

The Brightest Boughs

Underneath the shimmering lights,
Laughter dances through the nights.
The brightest boughs swaying free,
Nature sings a melody.

Twinkling stars above us shine,
Warming hearts with each design.
Joyful spirits filled with cheer,
Gathered close, we hold each dear.

Glistening treats and sweet delight,
Moments cherished, purest sight.
Beneath the boughs, we convene,
Creating memories serene.

With every hug and every song,
In this space, we all belong.
Together in love's gentle glow,
We celebrate the bonds we know.

Illuminated Soliloquy

Whispers soft in the cool night air,
As lights twinkle, the world laid bare.
Echoes of laughter fill the space,
Illuminated by joy's warm grace.

Fires crackle, stories unfold,
In this moment, magic's bold.
Sipping cider, hearts relate,
Sharing dreams while we celebrate.

Each flicker tells a tale so bright,
In shadows dancing, pure delight.
United in this glow we find,
A symphony of heart and mind.

Let this soliloquy resound,
In our hearts, love will abound.
With every glimmer, we will sing,
In this light, we feel the spring.

Dawn's Paintbrush

With each stroke, the dawn reveals,
Colors bright on the morning heals.
Soft pastels in the sky unfold,
A festive story, warm and bold.

Birds awaken, melodies play,
Nature calls with a bright display.
Joyful whispers ride the breeze,
In this moment, hearts at ease.

Sunshine breaking through the mist,
Every ray, a painter's twist.
As laughter dances on the dew,
Life unfolds, fresh and new.

Dawn's paintbrush in strokes divine,
Celebrates the love we find.
In this canvas, we embrace,
A festive world, a warm embrace.

Beacons of Nature

In the woods where laughter sings,
Joyful hearts spread their wings,
Bright blossoms dance in the breeze,
Nature's gifts put us at ease.

From the river, sparkles gleam,
Children play, lost in a dream,
Sunlight filters through the trees,
Warming spirits, hearts at ease.

Animals join in the cheer,
With each sound, the world draws near,
Whispers of the earth will call,
Inviting life, embracing all.

As night falls and stars ignite,
We gather round, hearts alight,
Together we share stories rare,
Beneath the moon, joy fills the air.

Shards of Sunshine

Golden rays in morning's wake,
Create a warmth that we partake,
Fields of buttercups sway along,
In this realm, we all belong.

Children's laughter rings so clear,
Joyful songs for all to hear,
Footprints left in soft, warm sand,
Echo the love in this land.

Picnics spread on checkered cloth,
Fruits and cakes that soothe the troth,
Sunsets glowing, colors bright,
Fill our hearts with pure delight.

As stars emerge, we dance around,
In every note, pure joy is found,
The night blooms with dreams so light,
In the warmth of soft twilight.

Woven in Light

Threads of gold in morning's burst,
Lighting up the world, a thirst,
For moments shared, smiles exchanged,
In this realm, nothing's estranged.

Crafting laughter, weaving glee,
In every heart, a melody,
Fires crackle, shadows play,
Echoes of the best of days.

Colors splashed in vibrant hues,
Each one tells a tale, renews,
Picnic blankets, stories shared,
Weaving bonds that none have bared.

As the moonlight softly glows,
We gather close, our spirits rose,
In this tapestry of night,
Forever wrapped, we hold the light.

Celestial Collectors

Gather 'round, let stories flow,
Under the sky's vast, jeweled show,
Stars above twinkle and gleam,
Whispering secrets in a dream.

Hearts alight with cosmic grace,
In this gathering, time finds its place,
Moonlit laughter, gleeful shouts,
Filling the night with joyful bouts.

Every soul a shining star,
Bringing warmth from near and far,
Tales of wonder, shared and bright,
In this moment, pure delight.

As dawn approaches, dreams will fade,
But memories linger, love is made,
In the echo of the cosmic dance,
We'll carry this joy—a timeless chance.

The Luminous Sanctuary

In the heart where laughter rings,
Candles flicker, joy it brings.
Strings of lights in vibrant hue,
Warmth and magic, all anew.

Friends gather with hearts so light,
Dancing shadows in the night.
Songs of cheer fill the cool air,
Memories weave, beyond compare.

Eager eyes and smiles that shine,
Every moment, bliss divine.
The stars above join in the cheer,
As love surrounds those gathered near.

With every toast, the spirits rise,
Underneath the starlit skies.
In this space, all cares are gone,
A luminous dance till the dawn.

Brilliance Beneath the Canopy

Underneath the sprawling trees,
Whispers carried by the breeze.
Lanterns twinkle, magic flows,
Bright with joy, the night glows.

Friends and laughter fill the air,
Joyful hearts, their love to share.
Charming tales and dreams unfold,
Glowing moments, bright and bold.

Nature sings a sweet refrain,
As spirits dance like falling rain.
Each glance exchanged, a spark ignites,
In this haven of starry nights.

Beneath the quilt of twinkling light,
We gather close, hearts feeling bright.
In this brilliance, hearts entwine,
Forever cherished, love's design.

Glowing Sanctum

In the glow of fireside cheer,
Voices blend, we hold most dear.
Wooden beams adorned with grace,
In this warm and sacred space.

Cheerful songs rise with the night,
Every smile a pure delight.
Mirthful eyes and stories spun,
In this sanctum, we are one.

Laughter dances on the breeze,
Every heart blooms like the trees.
In sweet moments, time holds still,
As we savor love's soft thrill.

With each embrace, our spirits soar,
In the glow, there's always more.
Here together, we ignite,
Endless joy in festive light.

Pathways of Radiance

Through the garden, lanterns gleam,
Guiding us like a sweet dream.
With each step, we laugh and play,
On this bright and joyful day.

Colors burst in every hue,
Nature's art, a wondrous view.
Hand in hand, we stroll along,
Hearts enchanted by the song.

Petals whisper in the night,
Under stars, a stunning sight.
Every glimmering path we trace,
Leads us deeper into grace.

At the end, a joyous cheer,
For together, we draw near.
In pathways lit, we find our way,
To celebrate this glorious day.

Celestial Blooms

Bright petals dance under the sun,
Colors singing, joy begun.
Butterflies waltz through fragrant air,
Nature's canvas, rich and rare.

Laughter rings from every tree,
Echoes of sweet harmony.
Gathered friends in merry cheer,
Celebrating, love is near.

Stars twinkle in twilight's glow,
Their soft whispers, gentle flow.
Buds unfold to greet the night,
A tapestry of pure delight.

Hands held high, we twirl and sway,
In this garden, we'll forever stay.
With each bloom, our spirits soar,
Celestial magic, forevermore.

Morning's Embrace

Golden rays peek through the trees,
A warm touch carried by the breeze.
Day awakens in soft hues,
Whispers of hope, the heart renews.

Birds flutter with joyous song,
Together where we all belong.
The world ignites with laughter's light,
A chorus singing, pure delight.

Crisp dewdrops on blades of grass,
Children racing, moments pass.
Underneath the sky so blue,
Every heartbeat feels brand new.

As the sun climbs high and bright,
Life unfolds in sheer delight.
Wrapped in warmth, we lift our gaze,
Morning's embrace, a gentle praise.

Chasing Dappled Shadows

Under trees where sunlight plays,
We weave through joy in merry ways.
Footsteps dance on sunlit ground,
Magic wraps us safe and sound.

Laughter flutters, a butterfly,
Chasing shadows as they fly.
Every corner, a secret kept,
In this moment, we feel blessed.

Picnics sprawled on blankets fine,
Sharing stories, sips of wine.
Sunset colors paint the skies,
In this realm, our spirits rise.

Together as the day will close,
With whispered dreams, our hearts compose.
Chasing dappled, sweet goodbye,
Joy forever, it shall not die.

Glistening Eden

In gardens bright where sunlight streams,
Each petal glistens, blooms like dreams.
Perfumed air ignites the soul,
A radiant tapestry, our goal.

Children laugh beneath the trees,
Chasing shadows in the breeze.
With every smile, joy's embrace,
In this Eden, we find grace.

Fireflies flicker, dance in night,
Guiding whispers, soft and bright.
Stars reflect on tranquil lakes,
A world alive, as joy awakes.

Together we sing, hearts entwined,
In this Eden, love defined.
With every moment, magic grows,
In glistening light, our spirit glows.

Nature's Beacon

Golden rays of morning light,
Dance upon the dew-kissed grass.
Butterflies take graceful flight,
Nature's whispers, sweet and fast.

Laughter echoes through the trees,
Joyful songs of birds arise.
Every moment, hearts at ease,
Underneath the azure skies.

Flowers bloom in vibrant hues,
Painting fields with pure delight.
Their fragrant, gentle scented views,
Make each day a wondrous sight.

As the sun begins to set,
Colors blend in perfect scene.
Nature's beacon, brightly met,
In this place, we're all serene.

The Shimmering Thicket

Through the thicket, sunlight streams,
Sparkling jewels on leaves so bright.
Nature's canvas, woven dreams,
Crafting magic, pure delight.

Children laugh and run in glee,
Chasing shadows, full of mirth.
Every laugh a melody,
Harmony upon the earth.

Petals flutter, fairies play,
In the shimmering, dappled light.
Joy awakens, come what may,
Transforming day into the night.

In this realm where hearts reside,
Whispers float on gentle breeze.
Here we find our joy and pride,
In the thicket, all is peace.

Dappled Sunlit Paths

Winding pathways draped in gold,
Sunlight dapples every step.
With each story gently told,
Nature's rhythm guides our prep.

Leaves are rustling, breezes stir,
Songs of crickets fill the air.
Moments cherished, nothing blur,
Smiles and laughter everywhere.

Flowers swaying to and fro,
Colors bright against the green.
In the sun's warm golden glow,
Every heart beats in between.

As we wander hand in hand,
Joyful memories we create.
Life unfolds, a dream so grand,
Dappled paths our hearts await.

Prism of Life

Catch the light in every hue,
Radiance of laughter gleams.
Moments shared, a lively crew,
Sailing softly on our dreams.

Candles flicker, spark the night,
Casting shadows, tales unfold.
In the warmth, a pure delight,
We gather round, our hearts consoled.

Bubbles rise like hopeful sighs,
Joy reflected in each gaze.
In this prism, laughter flies,
Filling nights with simple praise.

As the stars begin to glow,
We embrace the night divine.
In this quilt of love, we sew,
Life's sweet moments intertwine.

Glimmering Meadows

In fields where sunlight gleams,
The flowers sway with dreams,
Bright colors dance in the breeze,
Nature's joy puts hearts at ease.

Beneath the blue sky's embrace,
Laughter fills this sacred space,
Children play and spirits rise,
Echoes of cheer touch the skies.

Every corner bursts with cheer,
A festival of love draws near,
With every step, a song we hum,
In glimmering meadows, joy has come.

As twilight paints the day to rest,
Stars shimmer, a festive quest,
In this magic we unite,
Glimmering meadows, pure delight.

Stardust and Petals

Underneath a velvet sky,
Dreams and wishes soar and fly,
Petals drift on gentle streams,
Whispers of enchanted dreams.

Gathered here, hearts intertwined,
Love and laughter, sweetly kind,
Stardust sparkles in our eyes,
Underneath the twinkling skies.

A canvas bright with colors bold,
Stories of joy and warmth unfold,
Every moment, a treasure rare,
Together, magic fills the air.

Embracing night, we sing our song,
In stardust realms, we all belong,
With petals soft, our hopes ignite,
In this festival of pure delight.

Illuminated Paths

Through woods lit by lanterns bright,
We wander in the soft moonlight,
Each step a rhythm, every turn,
As warmth within our spirits burn.

Laughter echoes, friends draw near,
In this twilight, we feel no fear,
The path is lined with sparks of gold,
Adventures shared, memories bold.

Candles flicker, shadows play,
Guiding us along our way,
Every corner, a tale untold,
In illuminated paths of gold.

With every footfall, joy expands,
United here, hearts and hands,
Together we create the night,
Illuminated paths, pure delight.

A Dance of Colors

When sun rises and paints the sky,
Colors burst and spirits fly,
In petals bright and hues so bold,
A dance of colors unfolds.

Join the laughter, feel the cheer,
Every moment holds us near,
Hands entwined, we twirl and sway,
As vibrant tones sweep us away.

Balloons afloat like dreams on high,
Echoes of joy as we fly by,
In every shade, our hearts are free,
A dance of colors, harmony.

With every beat, the world does sing,
Celebrating what love can bring,
In this kaleidoscope of light,
A dance of colors, pure delight.

The Ethereal Grove

In the grove where laughter swirls,
Fairies dance in golden curls.
Breezes hum a joyous tune,
Underneath the silver moon.

Colorful lanterns gently sway,
As night embraces the end of day.
Whispers of magic fill the air,
Glimpses of joy everywhere.

Friends gather 'round the bonfire bright,
Sharing stories under starlight.
With every spark, our spirits soar,
In this grove, we want for more.

Let the night stretch on and on,
As we greet the soon-to-come dawn.
Together in this sacred place,
We find warmth, we find grace.

Sun-kissed Meadows

In sun-kissed meadows, flowers beam,
Children play and laughter streams.
Butterflies flutter, colors gleam,
Nature sings a joyful theme.

Picnics spread on blankets wide,
With friends and family by our side.
The scent of summer fills the air,
Creating memories we will share.

Dandelions dance in the breeze,
As we wish upon our knees.
A symphony of chirps and coos,
In sun-kissed meadows, we could lose.

The sun dips low, painting skies bright,
Our hearts are full, our spirits light.
Together we shall laugh and play,
In these meadows, come what may.

Glimmers of Serenity

In twilight's glow, the world unwinds,
Soft whispers of peace, the heart finds.
Gentle waves lap against the shore,
A calming rhythm we adore.

Moonlight casts a silver hue,
Nature's beauty, fresh and new.
Stars begin their nightly dance,
Inviting dreams with just a glance.

Candles flicker, shadows play,
As night unfolds, we choose to stay.
Each moment filled with pure delight,
Embracing calm, we hold it tight.

As dawn approaches, hearts in tune,
We bid farewell to the bright moon.
Yet glimmers of serenity remain,
In every laugh, in every gain.

Starry Fragrance

The night awakens with scents so sweet,
Beneath a sky where the cosmos meet.
Laughter dances on the evening air,
As we gather without a care.

Stars sprinkle magic on our dreams,
Guiding our hearts with gentle beams.
The fragrance of blossoms, fresh and rare,
Whispers of love linger everywhere.

Soft melodies float from afar,
Under the spell of the evening star.
Friends entwined in a cozy embrace,
Together, we savor this magical space.

As night unfolds its endless song,
We cherish the moments, joyful and strong.
For in this realm of starry grace,
We find our home, our sacred place.

Morning's Gentle Light

Morning breaks with colors bright,
Softly warming, pure delight.
Birds are singing, skies so clear,
Joyous laughter fills the sphere.

Flowers bloom in vibrant hues,
Dancing with the gentle dews.
Children playing, hearts so free,
In this moment, bliss we see.

Sunshine filters through the trees,
Whispers carried by the breeze.
Nature's chorus rings so true,
As a new day's dream breaks through.

Festive spirits, friends unite,
Underneath the golden light.
Together sharing smiles and cheer,
Embracing all that we hold dear.

Echoes of the Radiant

Echoes linger in the air,
Laughter dances everywhere.
Colors splash like joyful streams,
Filling hearts with vibrant dreams.

Rhythms pulse with every beat,
Life and love in harmony sweet.
Candles glowing, shadows play,
Creating magic in the sway.

Voices rise in melody,
Uniting souls in jubilee.
Moments treasured, pure and bright,
Echoing through the festive night.

Together we will weave the light,
Warming spirits, oh so bright.
Join the dance, the joyful song,
In this place where we belong.

Serene Lightfall

As the day begins to close,
Serene lightfall gently glows.
Stars awaken, twinkling high,
Underneath the painted sky.

Softly humming, night arrives,
Crickets singing, nature thrives.
Moonlight drapes the world in peace,
All our worries find release.

Gentle breezes kiss our skin,
Inviting dreams to dance within.
Whispers shared, and laughter true,
In this quiet, hearts renew.

With each twinkling star we see,
We feel the joy of unity.
Gathered 'neath this cosmic dome,
In the lightfall, we find home.

The Vibrant Oasis

In the desert, colors burst,
A vibrant oasis, quenching thirst.
Palm trees sway in soft embrace,
Nature's beauty, a sacred space.

Laughter dances with the breeze,
Joyful hearts find sweet release.
Underneath the azure skies,
Every moment feels like a prize.

Sun-kissed laughter, warm and bright,
Creating memories of pure delight.
In this haven, spirits soar,
Celebrating life, forevermore.

Together we will dance and sing,
In our oasis, let us bring.
Hands entwined, our dreams take flight,
In this vibrant, festive light.

The Bloom of Daydreams

In gardens bright with colors bold,
The whispers of the sun unfold.
Petals dance in joyful play,
As laughter fills the vibrant day.

With every breeze, the flowers sway,
Painting joy in sunlit array.
A symphony of scent and hue,
A dream alive in morning dew.

Beneath the sky, so deep and blue,
We gather hopes like blooms anew.
In this embrace of nature's cheer,
We find our heart, our vision clear.

So let us roam in nature's bliss,
In every moment, find the kiss.
The bloom of daydreams, bright and true,
A festive world awaits for you.

Echoes of Brilliance

In the twilight, stars ignite,
A symphony of joy takes flight.
Each sparkle tells a tale so bright,
Echoes of brilliance in the night.

Beneath the moon's soft, glowing gaze,
We dance in light, our spirits blaze.
With every step, the shadows fade,
In festive revels, memories made.

Voices mingle, laughter rings,
As the night to our hearts clings.
The air is filled with dreams so grand,
Together, side by side we stand.

The echo of our joy resounds,
In every heart, this magic found.
So grasp this moment, let it stay,
Echoes of brilliance lead the way.

Flora's Gentle Glow

In twilight's grace, the flowers bloom,
A gentle glow dispels the gloom.
Each petal shines with soft delight,
A festival of colors bright.

With whispered scents that fill the air,
We gather close, forgetting care.
The night is young, our spirits high,
Flora's light guides us through the sky.

In laughter's song, the moments blend,
As day to night, our hearts shall tend.
United here, in love's embrace,
A tapestry of joy we trace.

So let the blossoms dance and sway,
As we rejoice in this festive play.
In flora's glow, our dreams will soar,
Together always, forever more.

Twilight's Embrace

As twilight falls, the world ignites,
With softest hues of blues and whites.
The stars awaken, watch us gleam,
In festive glow, we share a dream.

The laughter spills like wine so sweet,
As hearts unite to drum a beat.
Under the stars, we find our place,
In twilight's arms, a warm embrace.

With every twinkle, joy aligns,
We weave together, hearts like vines.
In this moment, we are free,
Twilight's magic, you and me.

So raise a glass to paths we've crossed,
In twilight's dance, there's never loss.
Forever in this joyous glow,
Together, let our spirits flow.

Blossoms in the Sunlight

In gardens bright with colors bold,
The laughter dances, stories told.
With petals soft and fragrance sweet,
Each moment blooms, a joyous treat.

Children play beneath the trees,
As gentle whispers ride the breeze.
The sunlight glimmers on the dew,
A tapestry of vibrant hue.

The bees are humming, busy, wild,
In nature's arms, we are but children,
With love and laughter, we engage,
A beautiful and fleeting stage.

So raise a glass to days like this,
To nature's bounty, purest bliss.
With every smile, our hearts align,
In blossoms bright, the sun will shine.

Dawn's Gentle Embrace

The sky awakens, amber glow,
As dreams dissolve, the night will go.
The world is painted soft and light,
In dawn's embrace, the day feels right.

Birds sing sweetly, morning's song,
With hopeful hearts, we all belong.
The coffee brews, a cozy scent,
In every moment, time is spent.

The sun peeks through the open shade,
On dancing leaves, the light will wade.
A promise born with every ray,
In dawn's embrace, we greet the day.

So gather near and share the cheer,
In warmth of light, there's nothing to fear.
With every breath, feel joy expand,
And cherish each soft touch of hand.

Fragments of Light

Beneath the stars, we dance and twirl,
In moonlit dreams, our laughter swirls.
With every glance, a spark ignites,
In fragments of our joyful nights.

The music plays, the world awake,
Each heartbeat strong, our spirits shake.
With friend and kin, we weave our song,
In moments fleeting, where we belong.

The fire crackles, embers soar,
In this embrace, we seek for more.
With every story, hearts align,
In fragments bright, our souls entwine.

So lift your voice and let it ring,
In fragments of light, love is our spring.
Together we'll forge memories tight,
In every whisper, every light.

The Gleaming Countryside

The fields are gold, the skies are blue,
In countryside bliss, we wander through.
With laughter shared, the world expands,
In the gleaming light, we hold hands.

The sunflowers sway in rhythmic dance,
As breezes swirl in joyful prance.
With every step, the magic flows,
In the countryside, our spirit glows.

The winding paths and rustling leaves,
In nature's arms, our hearts believe.
With every glance, the beauty shines,
A canvas painted, love defines.

So let us roam where wildflowers bloom,
In every heartbeat, let joy resume.
In gleaming fields, our hopes arise,
Beneath the vast, enchanting skies.